AXOLOTL

Discovering the World's Most Adorable Animals

by **JESS KEATING**

with illustrations by DAVID DeGRAND

Alfred A. Knopf
New York

Think you know CUTE?

Turn the page to see some of the world's cutest animals in a whole new light. . . .

Cute as an AXOLOTL!

The **AXOLOTL** is one of the most adorable creatures around, but don't mistake it for just a cute face! These aquatic **salamanders** are masters of **regeneration.** If an axolotl loses a limb trying to escape a predator, it can simply grow it back. Sometimes it will even repair the damaged limb *and* grow a new one, leaving it with an extra arm or leg! As if that wasn't awesome enough, it can also regenerate its spine and jaws and parts of its *brain.*

Stylish Headgear!

See those feathery branches that grow from the sides of the axolotl's head? Those aren't just for show. They're the axolotl's gills! Unlike tadpoles, which lose their gills as they mature into frogs, healthy axolotls hang on to their gills for their entire lives.

Name: Axolotl (also called the Mexican walking fish)

Species name: *Ambystoma mexicanum*

Size: Up to 12 inches (30.5 centimeters), usually averaging 9 inches (22.9 centimeters)

Diet: Worms, insects and insect larvae, mollusks, crustaceans, other salamanders, and some fish

Habitat: The wet regions of Lake Xochimilco, near Mexico City

Predators and threats: Axolotls are listed as critically endangered, because their lake habitats are contaminated and drained often. Herons and **introduced species** like large fish lower their numbers, and they are also considered a delicacy in Mexico. Recent surveys have found no surviving individuals in the wild. Most breeding axolotls are now found in aquariums, research labs, and the pet trade.

Cute as a QUOKKA

With its perma-smile and fuzzy face, the **QUOKKA** is fast becoming one of the world's best-known cutie-pies. Tourists travel for miles just to get a quokka selfie! But is the quokka really smiling? Quokka scientists believe that that wide grin isn't *really* a smile—it's just the quokka's resting face. (But it's still pretty adorable.)

Watch Out—They Bite!

Rottnest Island, off the coast of Western Australia, is a popular spot to see quokkas. It's easy to love their smiling faces and plump bodies, but don't get too close. Quokkas are armed with sharp claws, and they have no problem taking a bite out of humans who get too close. Rottnest Island nurses treat several dozen painful quokka bites a year!

Name: Quokka

Species name: *Setonix brachyurus*

Size: 16–21 inches (40.6–53.3 centimeters), with a tail of roughly 9–12 inches (22.9–30.5 centimeters)

Diet: Swamp peppermint and other greenery

Habitat: The island swamps, riverbanks, thickets, and highly vegetated areas of Western Australia, and especially on Rottnest Island and Bald Island

Predators and threats: Quokkas are a huge tourist attraction and, as such, are vulnerable to human interference. Some quokkas get sick and die after being fed human food. Snakes, foxes, cats, dogs, and dingoes are their natural predators.

Cute as a FAIRY PENGUIN

Standing at roughly a foot tall, the **FAIRY PENGUIN** is the tiniest penguin on Earth. You might be familiar with the sight of penguins surrounded by snow, but these little guys live in mild, sunny regions on the southern coast of Australia and in New Zealand. Fairy penguins are also **diurnal,** heading out to sea at dawn under the cover of darkness. To further protect against predators, the little penguins always move together as a flock.

Small Penguin, Big Bodyguard

Not long ago, the fairy penguins of Warrnambool's Middle Island, off the southeastern coast of Australia, were in big trouble. A colony of 1,500 fairy penguins had been reduced to just four breeding pairs. What was responsible for these low numbers? Foxes. To protect the penguins, humans started the Maremma Project. Two **Maremma sheepdogs** were introduced as bodyguards for the penguins, and now their numbers are rebounding every day!

Name: Fairy penguin (also called the little penguin or little blue penguin)

Species name: *Eudyptula minor*

Size: Roughly 12–13 inches (30.5–33 centimeters), weighing 3.3 pounds (1.5 kilograms)

Diet: Small fish, such as anchovies and sardines, along with squid and krill

Habitat: The rocky coastlines of New Zealand, Tasmania, and Southern Australia

Predators and threats: Human interference in nest sites, car accidents, and habitat loss are all dangerous for the little penguins. They are also affected by plastic pollution (swallowing bottle rings, for example) and oil spills. Cats, dogs, foxes, rats, reptiles, ferrets, stoats, and other predators all hunt little penguins.

Cute as a POM-POM CRAB

What makes this **CRAB** cute? The pom-poms, of course! But you won't see these pom-poms at a football game—they are actually anemones. Each crab holds two anemones with its **chelipeds**, using them to ward off predators. If a hungry fish comes along, the crab wildly waves and shakes its "pom-poms" in the air.

CHOMP
CHOMP

CRUNCH
CHEW

Five-Second Rule!

The anemone pom-poms are not only handy to spook predators, but pom-pom crabs also use them to clean their homes and uncover tasty food. They "mop" their surroundings with the anemones, capturing scattered food particles. This is great for the crab, but also helps the anemones, who get to eat the leftovers! This type of win-win relationship is called **mutualism,** where both species benefit.

Name: Pom-pom crab (also called the boxer crab)

Species name: *Lybia tessellata*

Size: About 1 inch (2.5 centimeters) wide

Diet: This crab is a scavenger, feeding on small particles of fish and other scraps floating in the water.

Habitat: The sandy or gravelly seabeds, coral reefs, and shallow waters of the Indo-Pacific, spanning the East African coast and Red Sea region to Indonesia and New Guinea

Predators and threats: Birds, fish, turtles, octopuses, and even larger crustaceans are all predators of the pom-pom crab. As we see in coral reefs around the world, overfishing, tourism, and pollution threaten all the animals in the **ecosystem.**

Cute as a ROSY MAPLE MOTH

The **ROSY MAPLE MOTH** is one of the prettiest moths around, but that pink and yellow fuzz isn't just for looks. This moth is also an incredibly efficient **pollinator.** Every time the moth lands on a flower in its search for a mate, that coat of dense fuzz collects huge amounts of pollen. By transferring this pollen to other flowers, the moth helps plant species reproduce and survive.

Hungry? Too Bad!

Imagine if you could never eat for your entire adult life! The rosy maple moth, like many moths, does not eat once it reaches maturity. It doesn't even have a working mouth or **digestive system!** Instead, it survives off its fat, and spends most of its time trying to find a mate and reproduce. After mating, these moths die of starvation, but their **offspring** continue the cycle.

Name: Rosy maple moth

Species name: *Dryocampa rubicunda*

Size: Females are larger, with a wingspan of 1.5–2 inches (3.8–5.1 centimeters); males are roughly 1.25–1.75 inches (3.2–4.4 centimeters).

Diet: As caterpillars, they feed mainly on maple and oak leaves. As adults, they don't eat!

Habitat: The deciduous forests of North America, from northeastern Canada down the East Coast of the United States. They also live in areas of Michigan, Texas, Indiana, Kansas, and Nebraska.

Predators and threats: Many birds don't like to eat these moths because bright colors can be a warning sign of a bitter or toxic meal. However, blue jays, black-capped chickadees, and tufted titmice are all local predators.

Cute as a PANGOLIN

First things first. No, this is not a walking pinecone. The **PANGOLIN** is the world's only scaled mammal. These scales are made of **keratin**, which is the same stuff that makes up your hair and nails. But one of the coolest parts of the pangolin is hidden—its tongue, used for slurping insects, can be longer than its body! Unlike your tongue, which connects to the back of your mouth, the pangolin's tongue connects to its pelvis.

Tipping the Scales Against Animal Trafficking

Some cultures incorrectly believe that pangolin scales can cure cancer. The pangolin is also highly prized for its meat, blood, and other body parts. For this reason, it is one of the most heavily **trafficked** animals in the world. At least 10,000 pangolins are caught and sold illegally each year, and it's likely the real number is much, much higher. Happily, all eight species of pangolin are now protected by law.

Name: Chinese pangolin

Species name: *Manis pentadactyla*

Size: About 16–23 inches (40.6–58.4 centimeters) long, with a tail of 10–15 inches (25.4–38.1 centimeters)

Diet: Ants, termites, and other insects (especially larvae), as well as worms

Habitat: The limestone, bamboo, and tropical forests and grasslands of Bangladesh, Bhutan, Cambodia, China, Hong Kong, India, Laos, Myanmar, Nepal, the Philippines, Taiwan, Thailand, and Vietnam

Predators and threats: Pangolins are illegally traded around the world, so humans are a big threat to their survival. They also suffer from habitat loss, and all eight pangolin species are listed as either vulnerable or endangered.

Cute as a BARE-HEARTED GLASS FROG

Why call it the "BARE-HEARTED GLASS FROG"? The answer may be weirder than you think. This unique frog has transparent skin on its underside, so you can easily spot its heart, liver, and intestines from the outside! Imagine if you could see your lunch in your belly!

A Furtive Frog

At only an inch long, this frog eluded scientists for years. One reason for this is its tiny size, and it may have tricked our *ears* as well. The male bare-hearted glass frog sings at night to attract mates, but it sounds more like an insect than a frog. Don't let all the singing fool you, though. This frog is very **territorial,** and males will fight any frog that ventures too close to their homes.

Name: Diane's bare-hearted glass frog

Species name: *Hyalinobatrachium dianae*

Size: Roughly 1 inch (2.5 centimeters), with females being slightly larger

Diet: Soft-bodied insects and spiders

Habitat: The high elevations of approximately 1,300–2,600 feet (400–800 meters) in the Costa Rican rain forest and cloud forests

Predators and threats: Wild cats and other mammals, birds, and snakes are all enemies of most species of glass frogs. Global warming also threatens glass frogs, who rely on moist habitats and rain to survive. These frogs also suffer from pollution, habitat loss, and lethal fungus infections.

Cute as a PYGMY HIPPOPOTAMUS

This miniature mammal might look like a pint-size version of its larger cousin, but the **PYGMY HIPPO** is a creature all its own. Found in only four countries of West Africa, this forest-dwelling, bath-loving animal is nocturnal, spending most of its time noshing on leaves, roots, and fruit. When it does decide to swim, the pygmy hippo closes strong, muscular valves in its nose and ears to keep out water.

How Hippos Say Hi

Pygmy hippos are very shy, and they will usually avoid scuffles with other creatures. They are capable of making squeaks and grunts, but most pygmy hippos stay silent. Instead, they rely on body language to interact with each other. Much like dogs, pygmy hippos will lie on their backs to show another hippo they don't want to fight. They even wag their tails!

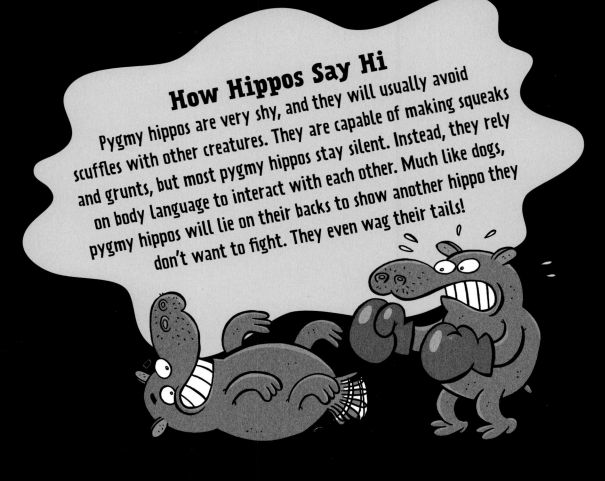

Name: Pygmy hippopotamus

Species name: *Choeropsis liberiensis*

Size: Roughly 4.9–5.7 feet (1.49–1.74 meters) long and 2.5–3.3 feet (76.2–100.6 centimeters) tall; they weigh anywhere from 397 to 606 pounds (180 to 275 kilograms).

Diet: Grasses, ferns, fruit, roots, and leaves

Habitat: The forests, swamps, wallows, and riverbeds of West Africa, including those in Liberia, Guinea, Sierra Leone, and the Ivory Coast

Predators and threats: Deforestation is the biggest threat to pygmy hippos, as they rely on forests and swamps to survive. They are also hunted by humans for meat. Leopards appear to be the only wild predator that adult hippos face, but young pygmy hippos are sometimes attacked by crocodiles and pythons.

Cute as a BEE FLY

It's a bee! It's a fly! No . . . it's a **BEE FLY**! This flying puffball gets its name from its remarkable resemblance to bees, though it is *all* fly. Its long, needle-like **proboscis** looks like a stinger, but the bee fly doesn't use it for defense. Instead, it uses it like a straw to suck up flower nectar, making this bee mimic harmless to humans.

Not-So-Innocent Babies

Grown bee flies enjoy nectar, but baby bee flies dine on more gruesome fare—they are **parasites** that eat the **larvae** of wasps, bees, and other insects that live in the ground. Mother bee flies hover near the nests of real bees, often flicking their eggs toward the entrance. When the bee fly babies are big enough, they sneak their way into the nest and attach themselves to a baby bee, ready to feed on it.

Name: Bee fly

Species name: *Bombylius major*

Size: Roughly 0.6–0.7 inch (1.5–1.8 centimeters)

Diet: As larvae, bee flies are parasites, feeding on the food stores of their host insects or on the insect grubs (babies). As adults, they drink nectar from flowers.

Habitat: Bee flies are very common, found in temperate regions in every continent except Antarctica. They are usually seen in spring, when they are feeding on early-spring flowers or looking for bee nests to hide their larvae in.

Predators and threats: Frogs, birds, and larger insects are all potential predators, but bee flies are often avoided because of their bee-like appearance. Habitat loss is a threat for bee flies, so nature reserves offer vital protection for these important pollinators.

Cute as a DWARF FLYING SQUIRREL

What has an adorable face and some epic flight gear? Meet the JAPANESE DWARF FLYING SQUIRREL. Despite its name, it can't really fly. Rather, it employs a membrane called a **patagium,** which stretches like wings between its front paws and its ankles. This allows it to leap into the air, gliding from tree to tree. By gliding, this squirrel can cover huge distances in the air.

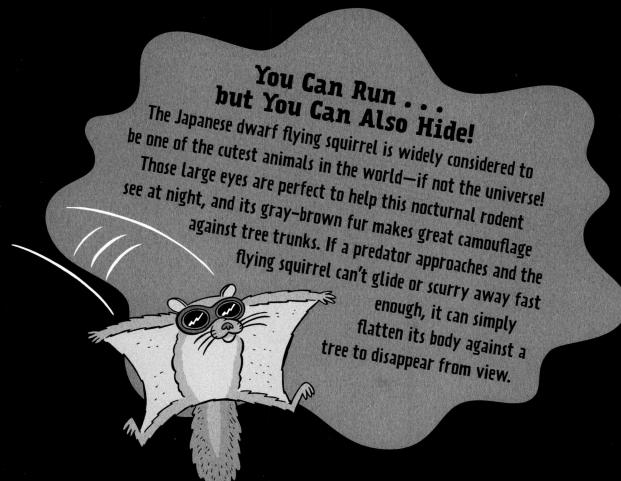

You Can Run . . . but You Can Also Hide!

The Japanese dwarf flying squirrel is widely considered to be one of the cutest animals in the world—if not the universe! Those large eyes are perfect to help this nocturnal rodent see at night, and its gray-brown fur makes great camouflage against tree trunks. If a predator approaches and the flying squirrel can't glide or scurry away fast enough, it can simply flatten its body against a tree to disappear from view.

Name: Japanese dwarf flying squirrel

Species name: *Pteromys momonga*

Size: About 8 inches (20.3 centimeters) in length

Diet: Seeds, fruit, buds, leaves, and tree bark

Habitat: The northern forests of Japan, especially Honshu and Kyushu islands. Japanese dwarf flying squirrels usually make their homes in the cavities of conifer trees.

Predators and threats: There are not many known predators of these flying squirrels, but owls could be a threat. As with all **arboreal** animals, deforestation impacts their numbers.

Cute as a BLUE DRAGON

Nope, it's not a figment of your imagination or a character in a video game. The **BLUE DRAGON** is the real deal, and shares its scientific name with the ancient Greek sea god Glaucus. This squishy blue **nudibranch** could sit on your fingertip, but don't touch it! The blue dragon eats venomous creatures like the Portuguese man-of-war. But instead of getting sick, it stores their venom in its skin and becomes toxic itself.

Now You See Me • • •

The blue dragon may look beautiful, but its bright colors and striking patterns serve a purpose. When viewed from above, its blue back blends in with the water. When seen from below, its silvery gray underside looks just like the sunlit waves. This type of camouflage is called **countershading,** and can also be seen in certain species of sharks and whales.

Name: Blue dragon (also called the sea swallow or blue sea slug)

Species name:
Glaucus atlanticus

Size: 1.2 inches (3 centimeters)

Diet: Other animals that live in the open sea (**pelagic zone**), including the Portuguese man-of-war

Habitat: The temperate and tropical waters of South Africa, Mozambique, Europe, and Australia. They have also been found near India and Peru and along the western Atlantic coast. Blue dragons are usually found in the open ocean, but they sometimes wash ashore on beaches. They can still produce a painful sting even *after* they're dead, so steer clear!

Predators and threats: Because of their stinging cells, these nudibranchs are not often targeted by predators. **Climate change** and **ocean acidification** both pose threats to this species.

Cute as a DIK-DIK

The **DIK-DIK** is one of the world's smallest antelopes, standing just over a foot tall. It makes its home in parts of eastern Africa, where the weather can grow very hot. To stay cool, the dik-dik is armed with a special proboscis. By panting through this enlarged nose, dik-diks cool off quickly! Curious about that weird name? The dik-dik is named for the squeaky alarm call females make when disturbed.

Don't Waste Those Tears!

Some animals mark their territory with urine or scat (poop). Dik-diks do, too, but they also use their tears! Or, more specifically, fluid from a gland in the corner of their eyes called the **preorbital gland.** By wiping the gland and its fluid over grass and tree leaves near their home, dik-diks tell other dik-diks: this is *my* home!

Name: Kirk's dik-dik

Species name:
Madoqua kirkii

Size: Roughly 12–16 inches (30.5–40.6 centimeters) at the shoulder

Diet: Low-lying grass, shrubs, and leaves. Often, the only water they consume comes from vegetation or dew found on grasses.

Habitat: The arid regions of southeastern Somalia, southern and central Kenya, northern and central Tanzania, southwestern Angola, and Namibia, where there is lots of shrubbery for protection

Predators and threats: Humans sometimes hunt dik-diks for their **pelts,** which are used to make gloves. They are also hunted by lions, leopards, cheetahs, caracals, genets, jackals, hyenas, crocodiles, pythons, baboons, and eagles. Their habitat is also in decline due to deforestation and **slash-and-burn agriculture.**

Cute as a PYGMY RABBIT

Nearly two decades ago, **PYGMY RABBITS** were nearly **extinct,** with only thirty animals found in the wild. Thanks to captive-breeding programs, these little bundles of fur are making a slow rebound. To protect their babies, female pygmy rabbits bury them in shallow burrows, using their long claws to dig into the ground. After a day of eating, the females return and unbury their kids, nurse them, and rebury them again. This lasts for two weeks, until the baby rabbits can fend for themselves.

Little Bunnies, Strong Stomachs

Pygmy rabbits are the smallest rabbits in the world. They survive by eating sagebrush leaves, which can make up to 100 percent of their diet in winter. These leaves are bitter and toxic to many animals, including humans. The rabbits are able to digest them because they have larger livers than most rabbits. Their livers remove the toxins from the leaves, and the rabbits enjoy their meal without getting sick.

Name: Pygmy rabbit

Species name: *Brachylagus idahoensis*

Size: Roughly 9–11.6 inches (22.9–29.5 centimeters)

Diet: Mainly sagebrush in the winter, along with grasses in the summer

Habitat: The unforested sagebrush regions of Washington State, as well as areas of California, Idaho, Montana, Nevada, Oregon, and Wyoming

Predators and threats: Sagebrush is very sensitive to fire, so forest fires and **controlled burning** can pose a problem for these creatures. Deforestation and farming are also dangerous for them, as they remove sagebrush and create looser, sparser soil that makes burrowing very difficult. Weasels, hawks, foxes, bobcats, badgers, coyotes, and owls are all natural predators.

Cute as a MINUTE LEAF CHAMELEON

Measuring just over an inch long, the MINUTE LEAF CHAMELEON is easy to miss—but hard to forget. It lives only in a small region of Madagascar, where it forages in leaf litter for food. In the trees, this chameleon is always looking out for predators. If its branch is shaken or moved, it will drop to the ground like a piece of dead wood and stay still until the threat is gone.

Dainty Dwarfs on Isolated Islands

There are several species of leaf chameleons, many of which are incredibly small. But how did they get that way? The answer might be related to their homes. Scientists believe that some species get tinier over time if they live on a small island with limited food and space. This is called **insular dwarfism.** Leaf chameleons are one of many miniaturized animals in Madagascar, along with dwarf lemurs and the extinct Malagasy dwarf hippos.

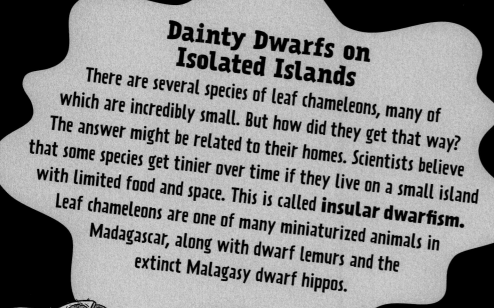

Name: Minute leaf chameleon (also called the Madagascan dwarf chameleon)

Species name: *Brookesia minima*

Size: Up to 1.1 inches (2.8 centimeters) in males and 1.3 inches (3.3 centimeters) in females

Diet: Small fruit flies, white flies, and springtails (small insects that live in leaf litter)

Habitat: The leaf litter and dead leaves of the evergreen rain forest in isolated regions of Madagascar, including Nosy Be island

Predators and threats: Snakes and birds are the main predators of these chameleons, but mammals like ringtail lemurs might eat them if given the chance. These animals are threatened by mining, agriculture, and other sources of habitat destruction. As with many Madagascan species, conservation is needed to protect their homes.

Cute as a SAW-WHET OWL

With their huge, bright eyes and teeny stature, SAW-WHET OWLS are the cutest things on wings in the forest, and no stranger to awesome adaptations. All owls share a superpower: their wings are almost completely silent in flight. Specialized feathers reduce noise, first by dispersing **turbulence.** Then the downy feather edges absorb the remaining noise. That's one stealthy bird!

Love Birds

Northern saw-whet owls are usually **monogamous,** which means they have one mate at a time. When a male saw-whet owl wants to woo a female, it will call out and sing a song. If a female is interested, she'll call back. They will spend the year together, raising a brood of chicks. Sometimes they even preen each other's feathers!

Name: Northern saw-whet owl

Species name:
Aegolius acadicus

Size: 6.7–8.7 inches (17–22.1 centimeters)

Diet: Small mammals, such as deer mice, voles, shrews, bats, and young squirrels, as well as small birds and large insects

Habitat: These owls breed in the coniferous and deciduous forests across North America, and spend their winters in the central and southern United States.

Predators and threats: Larger owls, martens, and hawks are natural threats to these owls, and they also compete for resources with starlings, squirrels, and boreal owls. Because they use different areas of the forest at different times of their life, forest conservation is crucial to their survival.

Cute as a HUMMINGBIRD BOBTAIL SQUID

It's a vibrant rainbow of colors, but the **HUMMINGBIRD BOBTAIL SQUID** spends most of its time hiding right before your eyes. Shimmying and shifting, it uses its arms and tentacles to cover itself with loose sand on the ocean floor, leaving only its eyes exposed. Once hidden, it stays protected from predators and waits to pounce on unsuspecting prey.

A Light in the Dark

How do you stay hidden in the water when you're out hunting? You get a little help from your friends! These squid have bioluminescent bacteria that live in their **mantle.** The bacteria are fed by the squid, and in return, they adjust their light to match the moonlight, which beams on the squid at night while they hunt. This is known as **counter-illumination.**

Name: Hummingbird bobtail squid

Species name: *Euprymna berryi*

Size: Females reach roughly 2 inches (5.1 centimeters) in length; males are smaller, at 1.2 inches (3 centimeters).

Diet: Small **benthic** crustaceans and small fish

Habitat: The sandy ocean floors of warm tropical waters in the central Indo-Pacific area, ranging from Indonesia to the Philippines, southern Japan, and the coast of China, including Taiwan

Predators and threats: Many predatory fish enjoy eating squid, including sharks and rays. Humans also routinely catch and eat these animals, but very little is known about how these practices affect their numbers.

Cute as a FENNEC FOX

This big-eared cutie may be adorable, but the **FENNEC FOX** is perfectly adapted to its environment. Those giant six-inch ears help this creature survive some of the hottest regions on Earth by radiating extra body heat to keep the fox cool. Their ears are also remarkable hunting tools. By tilting its head in different directions, the fennec fox can pinpoint small animals moving under the sand. One quick dig and dinner is served!

No Water? No Worries!

When you get hot, it's important to drink water to survive. But the fennec fox is so well adapted to the hot desert, it can live without freestanding water. That means it *never* needs to drink from streams or watering holes. Instead, it gets water from the food it eats. It also laps up dew that collects in its deep burrows and dens.

Name: Fennec fox

Species name: *Vulpes zerda*

Size: 9–16 inches (22.9–40.6 centimeters) in length, with a tail of roughly 7–12 inches (17.8–30.5 centimeters), standing about 8 inches (20.3 centimeters) tall

Diet: Fruit, plants, insects, rodents, reptiles, birds, eggs, and some smaller mammals like rabbits

Habitat: The sandy, arid regions of North Africa and Asia, from Morocco to Egypt, down to northern Niger, and eastward toward the Sinai Peninsula and Kuwait

Predators and threats: The fennec fox has many predators, including striped hyenas, jackals, and eagle owls. They are also often trapped by humans looking to sell them into the pet trade or for their fur.

The Science of Cute

Have you ever thought about what makes a certain animal cute?
Believe it or not, cuteness could be a survival strategy.

Scientists believe that animals with large eyes and high foreheads, rounded faces, small noses, and plump bodies appear especially cute to us. It's possible we think these traits are cute because we see them in our own human babies. Humans need to take care of their babies for a long time, and some scientists believe that cute babies help us develop a bond with our offspring. Do wild animals see their kids as cute? More research is needed to answer this question.

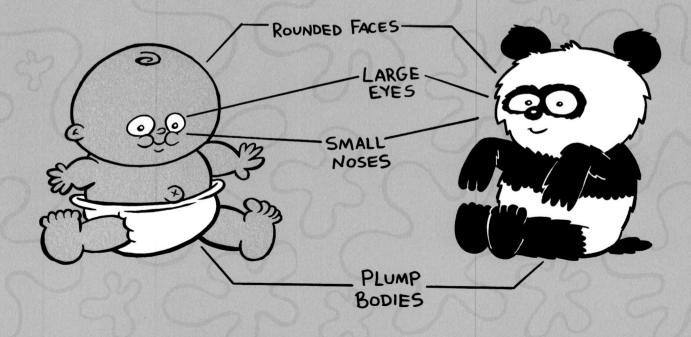

ROUNDED FACES

LARGE EYES

SMALL NOSES

PLUMP BODIES

Animators and illustrators think about what's "CUTE" every day. They design characters to be as cute as possible so you will like them more!

Try examining animals in this book. Which seems the CUTEST to you? What FEATURES does it have? What is the LEAST CUTE animal in the book? Does this surprise you? What about your own FAVORITES that didn't make it into the book? What FEATURES do they share?

Grab a pencil and paper and try drawing YOUR VERSION of a cute animal. Use the TRAITS you think are cutest from the examples on the previous page, or from the animals you found in the book. Compare your creation with real-life animals, or one that a friend or classmate has drawn. How do your CUTE CREATIONS differ? Which is cutest? Can you pinpoint the TRAITS that make you think this way?

We are more likely to HELP CUTE ANIMALS and protect their homes in the wild. Do you think this is FAIR?

Say What?! A Glossary of Useful Words

Some of the words in the text are in **bold**. If you didn't understand them,
you can use the list below to learn their definitions.

- **Arboreal:** living mainly in trees
- **Benthic:** occurring on the lowest, deepest level in a body of water, including the ocean floor
- **Chelipeds:** legs with a pincer-like claw called a chela, found in arthropods such as crabs
- **Climate change:** when the temperature of the Earth's atmosphere and oceans changes (for example, grows warmer), affecting animals, plants, and humans
- **Controlled burning:** setting small, carefully managed fires to keep a forest healthy and prevent larger, uncontrolled fires
- **Counter-illumination:** producing light to match a background, as a form of camouflage
- **Countershading:** having darker colors on top and lighter ones underneath, as a form of camouflage
- **Deforestation:** the process of clearing forests by logging or burning trees
- **Digestive system:** a group of organs working together to break down food and convert it to energy
- **Diurnal:** active mainly during the day
- **Ecosystem:** a community of organisms functioning as a unit with their environment
- **Extinct:** no longer existing in the world

- **Insular dwarfism:** the process by which animals become smaller over several generations due to living in a restricted environment, like an island
- **Introduced species:** species that are not originally from a given area, but are brought there by humans
- **Keratin:** a protein that is found in numerous animals, forming hair, nails, hooves, feathers, and claws
- **Larvae:** the young of some animals, such as frogs, insects, and jellyfish, that go through drastic physical changes as they grow up
- **Mantle:** the soft, colored tube that forms the main part of a mollusk's body
- **Maremma sheepdog:** a large breed of dog, originally bred in Italy for guarding flocks of sheep
- **Monogamous:** having only one mate at a time
- **Mutualism:** a relationship that benefits both of the organisms involved
- **Nudibranch:** a shell-less marine mollusk, also called a sea slug
- **Ocean acidification:** the process by which the oceans are becoming more acidic, caused by increased levels of gases, such as carbon dioxide, in the atmosphere
- **Offspring:** an animal's young

- **Parasite:** an organism that lives on or in another organism (called its host), obtaining nourishment at the expense of its host
- **Patagium:** a membrane or fold of skin between the forelimbs and hind limbs of gliding mammals or bats
- **Pelagic zone:** the part of the open ocean or sea that is not near the coast or seafloor
- **Pelt:** the hair, fur, or wool of an animal, along with its skin, when removed from the animal
- **Pollinator:** an animal that transfers pollen from the male parts of a flower to the female parts of a flower
- **Preorbital gland:** a gland found in the corner of the eyes of some hoofed animals that helps them mark their territory
- **Proboscis:** in insects, a long, flexible sucking mouthpart; in mammals, a long and sometimes mobile nose

- **Regeneration:** the process by which animals or plants replace lost or damaged parts by growing them again
- **Salamander:** a group of amphibians with slender bodies, blunt snouts, and short limbs
- **Slash-and-burn agriculture:** a method of agriculture that involves cutting down trees and burning the remaining vegetation, mainly used in tropical regions
- **Territorial:** defending an area against intruders, especially of the same species
- **Trafficked:** dealt or traded in something illegal
- **Turbulence:** a disturbance of air that may ruffle a bird's wings and produce noise

THIS IS A BORZOI BOOK PUBLISHED BY ALFRED A. KNOPF   Text copyright © 2018 by Jess Keating   Jacket art and interior illustrations copyright © 2018 by David DeGrand
All rights reserved. Published in the United States by Alfred A. Knopf, an imprint of Random House Children's Books, a division of Penguin Random House LLC, New York.
Knopf, Borzoi Books, and the colophon are registered trademarks of Penguin Random House LLC.

Visit us on the Web! rhcbooks.com   Educators and librarians, for a variety of teaching tools, visit us at RHTeachersLibrarians.com

Library of Congress Cataloging-in-Publication Data is available upon request.
ISBN 978-1-5247-6447-0 (trade) — ISBN 978-1-5247-6448-7 (lib. bdg.) — ISBN 978-1-5247-6449-4 (ebook)

The illustrations in this book were created using ink and digital coloring.
MANUFACTURED IN CHINA   August 2018   10 9 8 7 6 5 4 3 2 1   First Edition
Random House Children's Books supports the First Amendment and celebrates the right to read.